PHOTO ALBUM

Belongs to

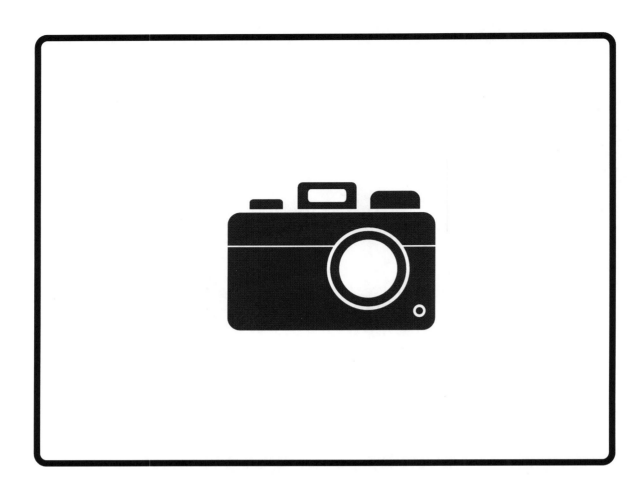

Place

Date   Title

Notes

Place

Title

Date

Notes

Place ———————————

Date ——————— Title ———————

Notes

Place

Title

Date

Notes

Place

Date Title

Notes

Place

Title

Date

Notes

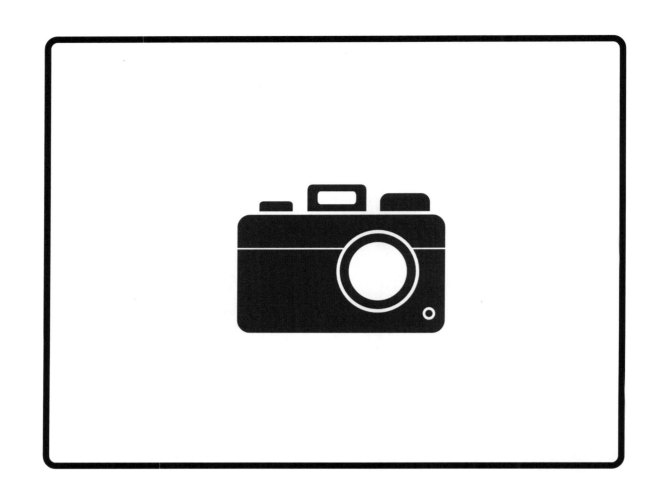

Place

Date　　　　　Title

Notes

Place _____

Title _____

Date _____

Notes

_____
_____
_____
_____

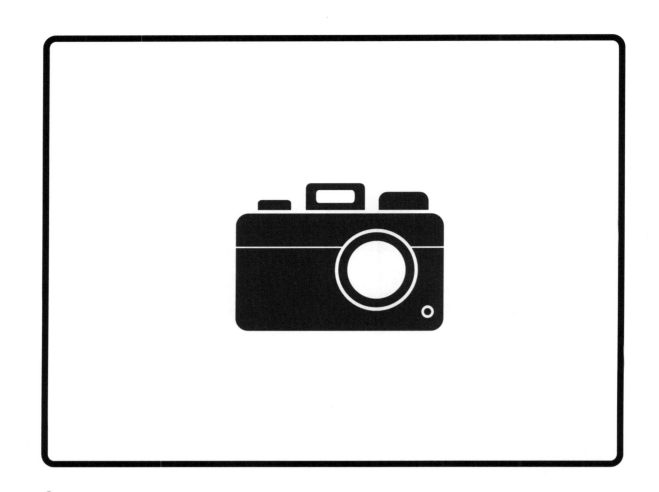

Place

Date Title

Notes

Place

Title

Date

Notes

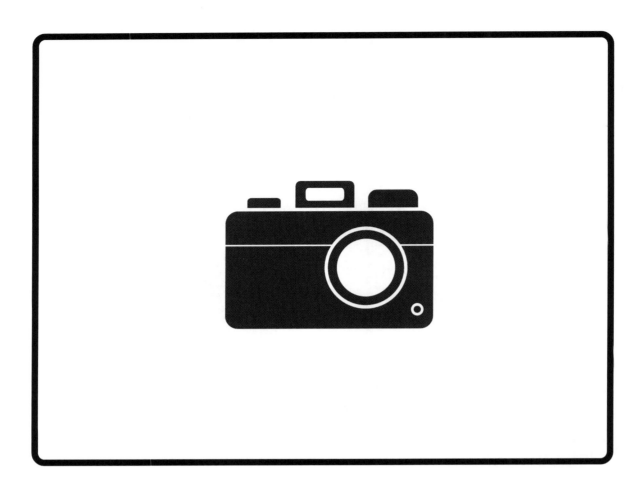

Place

Date　　　　　Title

Notes

Place

Title

Date

Notes

Place

Date　　　　　　　Title

Notes

Place _____

Title _____

Date _____

Notes

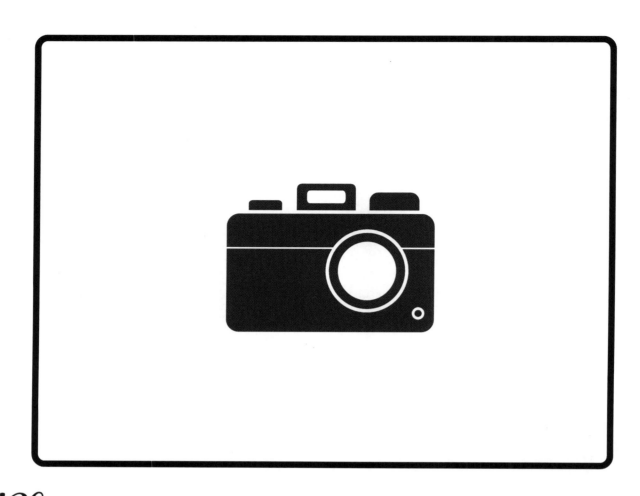

Place

Date Title

Notes

Place

Title

Date

Notes

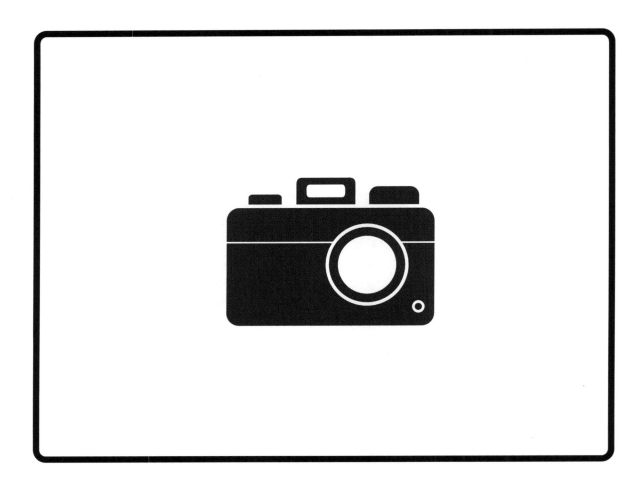

Place

Date Title

Notes

Place

Title

Date

Notes

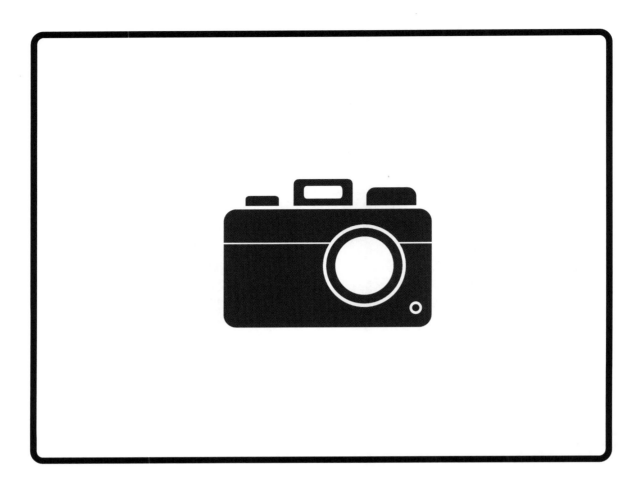

Place

Date　　　　　　Title

Notes

Place

Title

Date

Notes

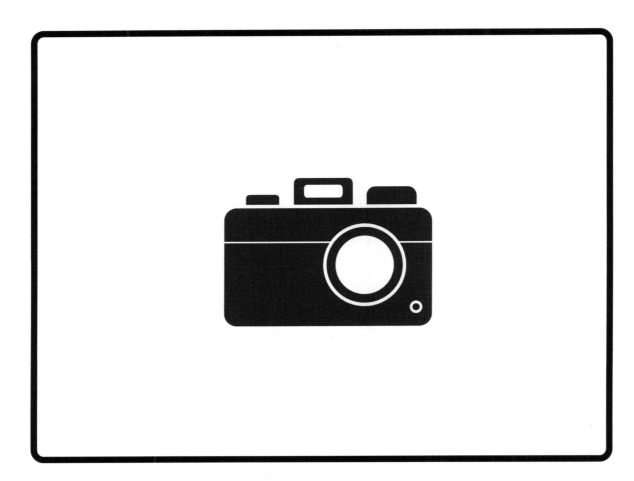

Place

Date　　　　　　　　Title

Notes

Place

Title

Date

Notes

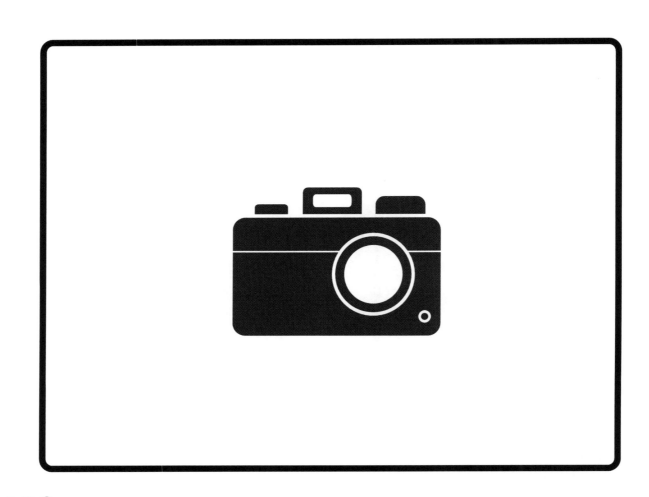

Place

Date Title

Notes

Place

Title

Date

Notes

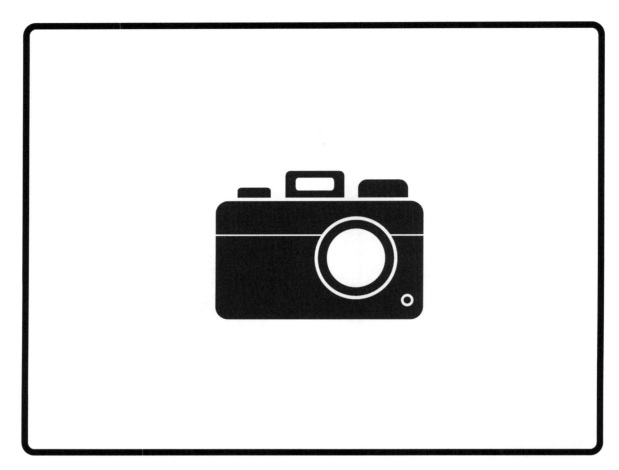

Place

Date　　　　　Title

Notes

Place _____

Title _____

Date _____

Notes

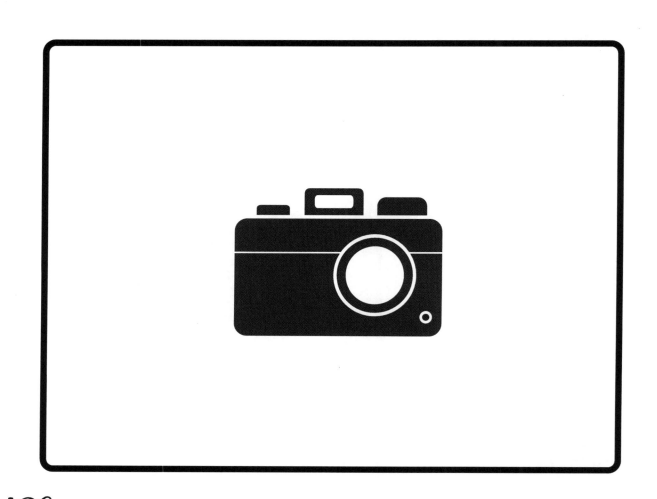

Place _____

Date _____ Title _____

Notes

Place

Title

Date

Notes

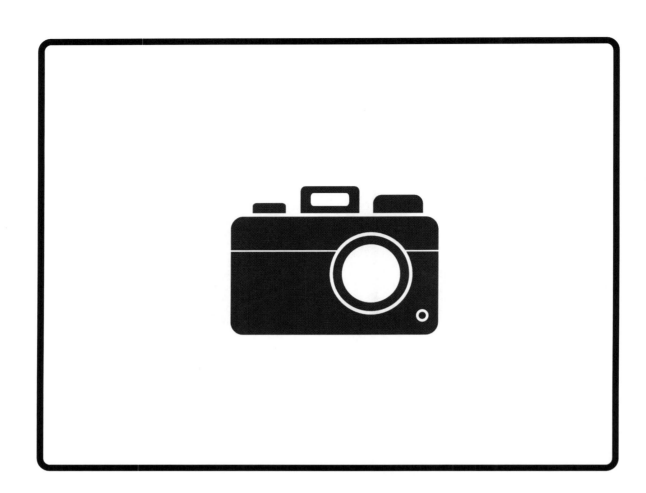

Place

Date Title

Notes

Place

Title

Date

Notes

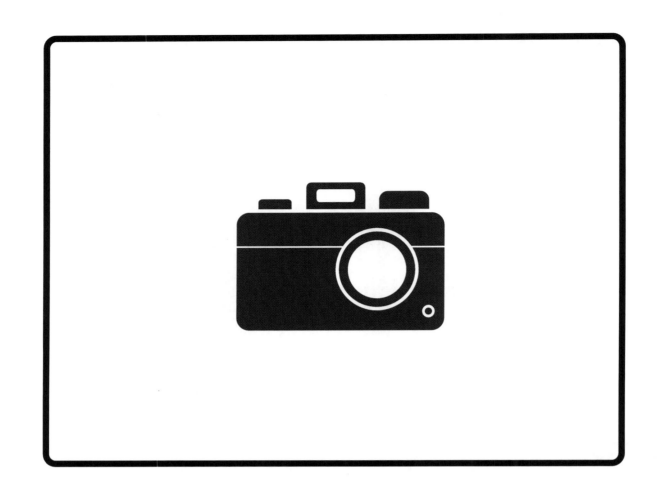

Place

Date　　　　　　　Title

Notes

Place

Title

Date

Notes

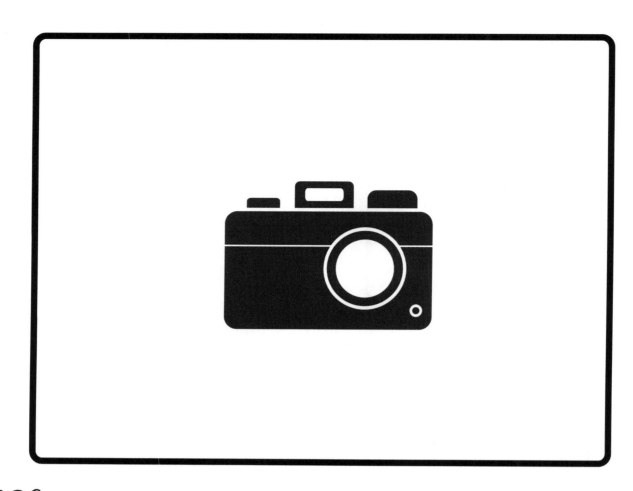

Place

Date　　　　　　　Title

Notes

Place _____

Title _____

Date _____

Notes

Place

Date Title

Notes

Place

Title

Date

Notes

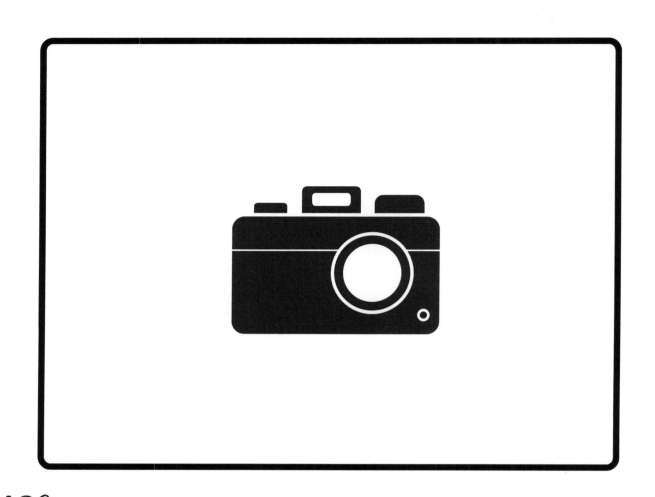

Place

Date Title

Notes

Place

Title

Date

Notes

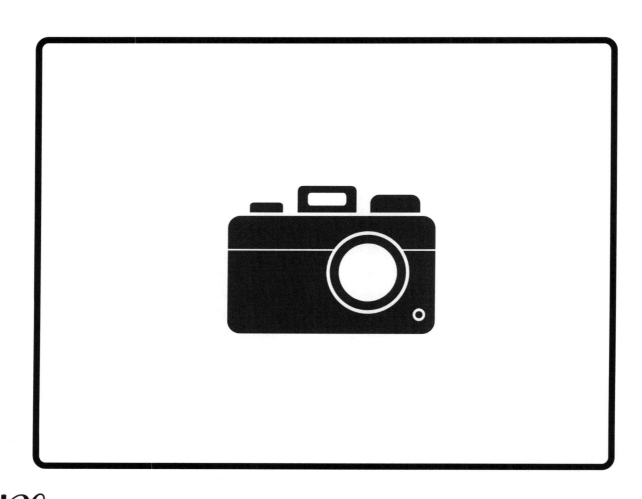

Place

Date Title

Notes

Place

Title

Date

Notes

Place

Date   Title

Notes

Place

Title

Date

Notes

Place

Date　　　　　　　Title

Notes

Place

Title

Date

Notes

Place

Date Title

Notes

Place

Title

Date

Notes

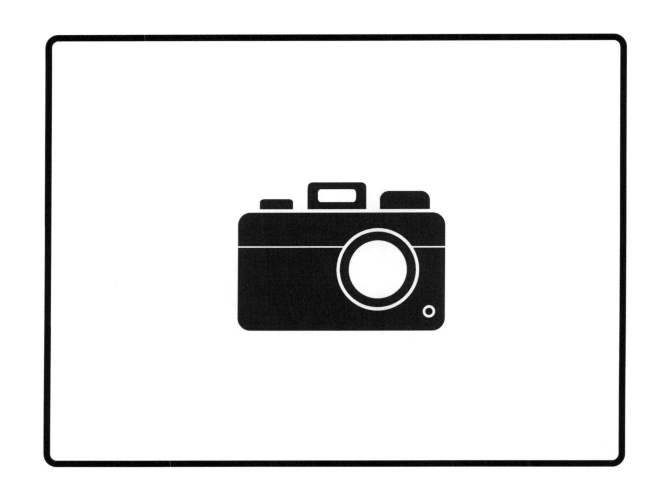

Place

Date　　　　　　　Title

Notes

Place

Title

Date

Notes

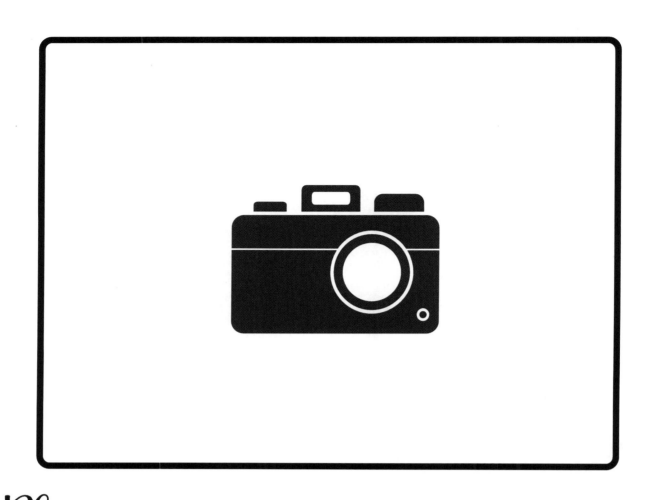

Place

Date Title

Notes

Place

Title

Date

Notes

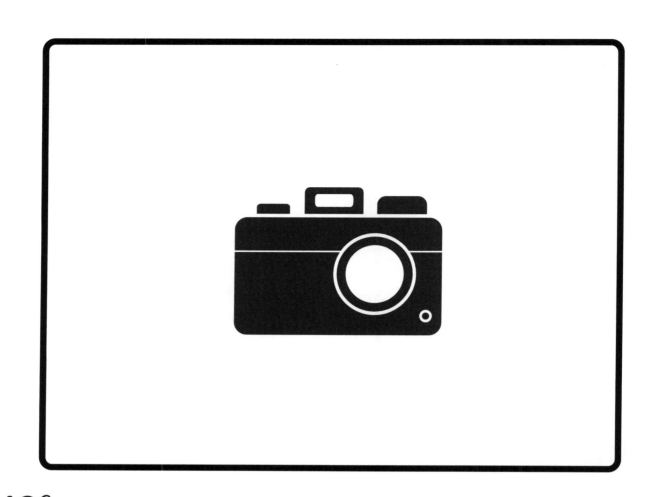

Place

Date Title

Notes

Place

Title

Date

Notes

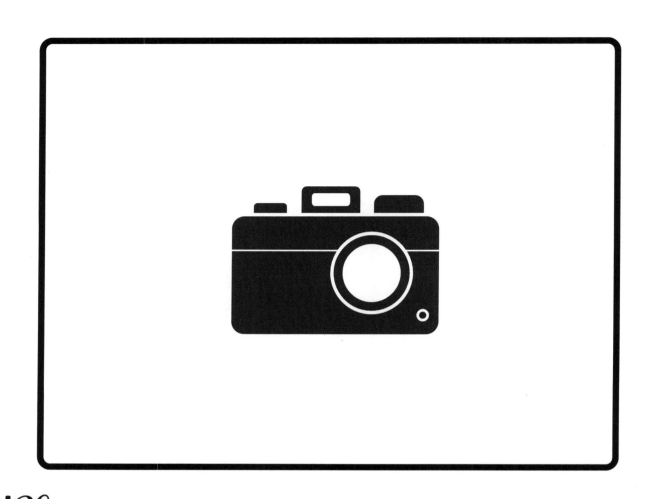

Place

Date Title

Notes

Place

Title

Date

Notes

Place

Date　　　　　　Title

Notes

Place

Title

Date

Notes

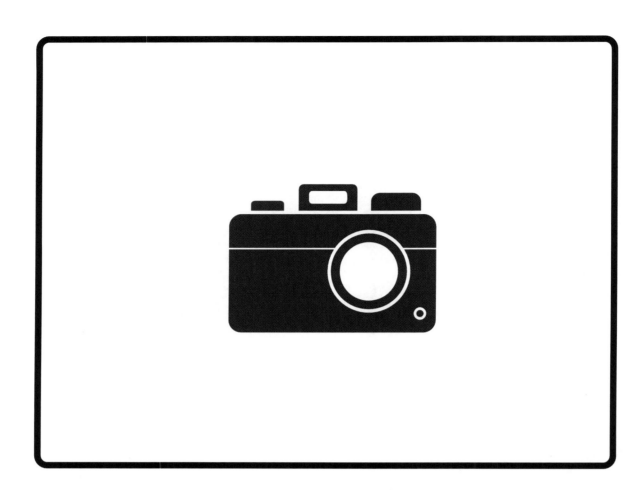

Place

Date   Title

Notes

Place

Title

Date

Notes

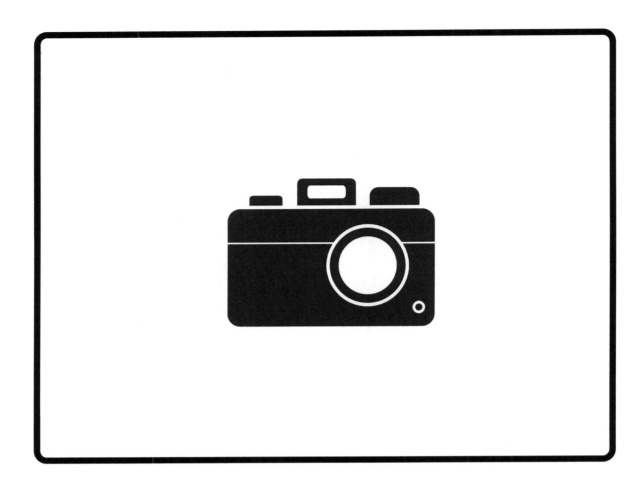

Place

Date   Title

Notes

Place

Title

Date

Notes

Place

Date　　　　　　Title

Notes

Place

Title

Date

Notes

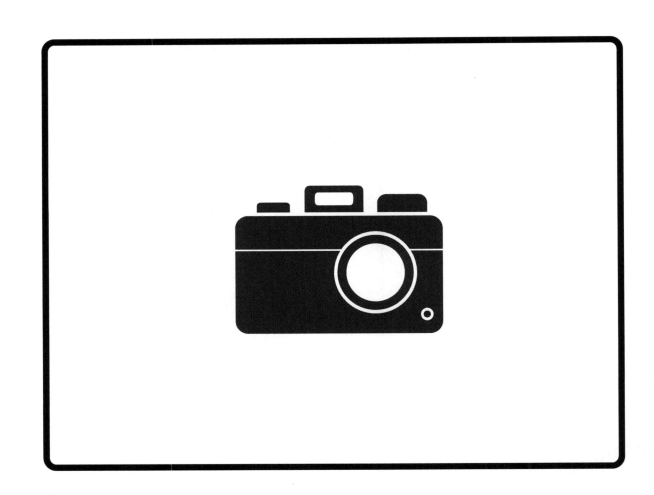

Place

Date Title

Notes

Place

Title

Date

Notes

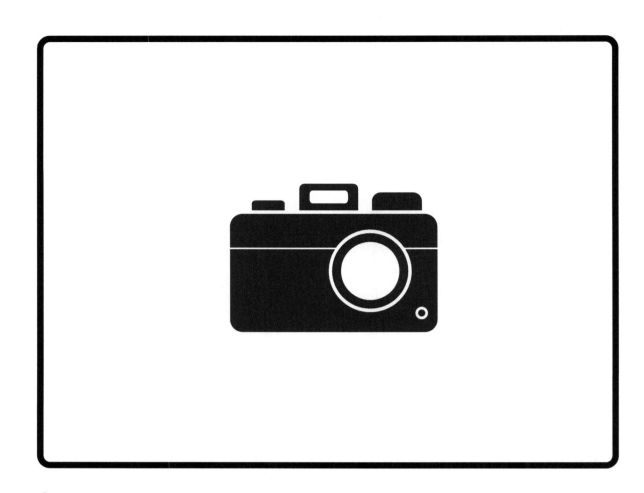

Place
Date   Title

Notes

Place

Title

Date

Notes

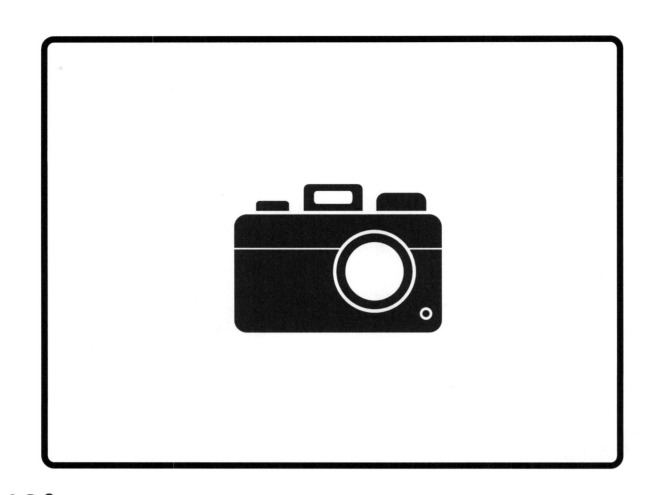

Place
Date Title

Notes

Place

Title

Date

Notes

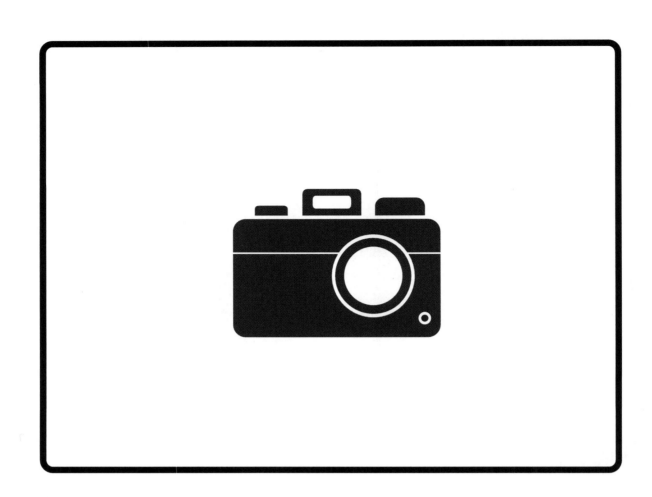

Place _____

Date _____ Title _____

Notes

_____
_____
_____
_____
_____

Place

Title

Date

Notes

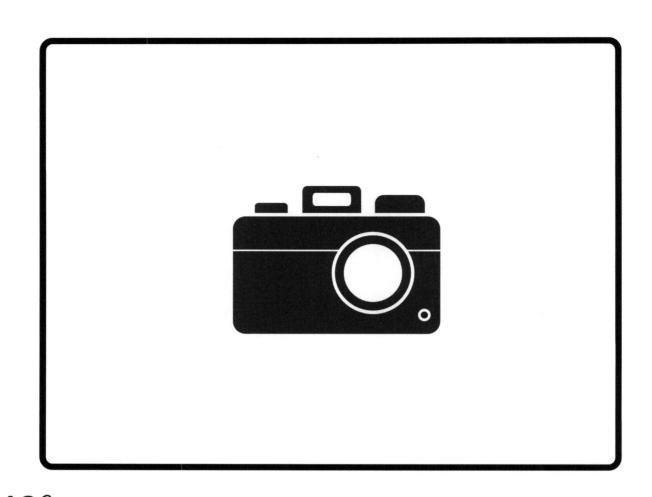

Place _____

Date _____ Title _____

Notes

_____
_____
_____
_____
_____

Place

Title

Date

Notes

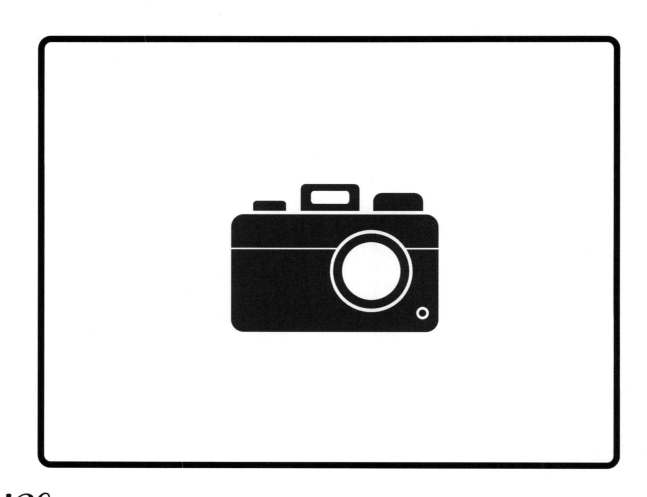

Place _____

Date _____ Title _____

Notes

_____

_____

_____

_____

_____

Place

Title

Date

Notes

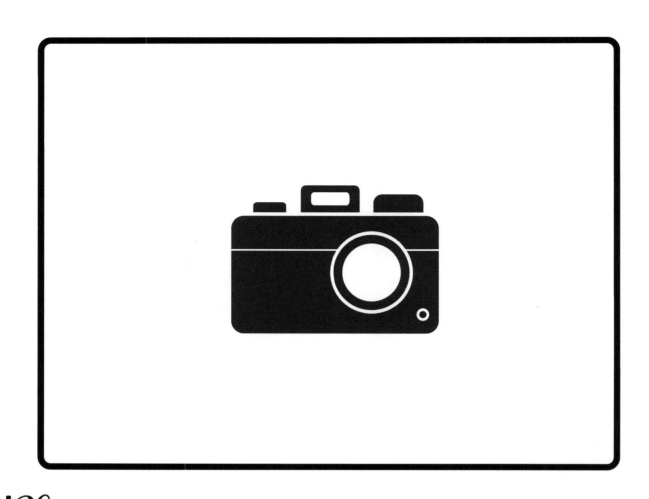

Place

Date　　　　　　　　Title

Notes

Place

Title

Date

Notes

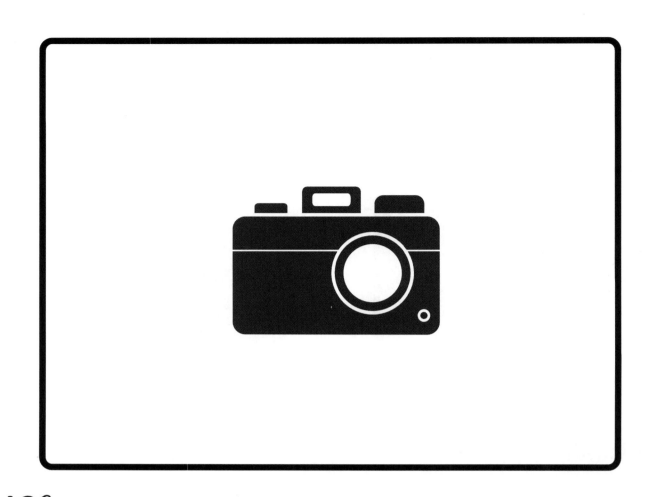

Place _____

Date _____ Title _____

Notes

Place

Title

Date

Notes

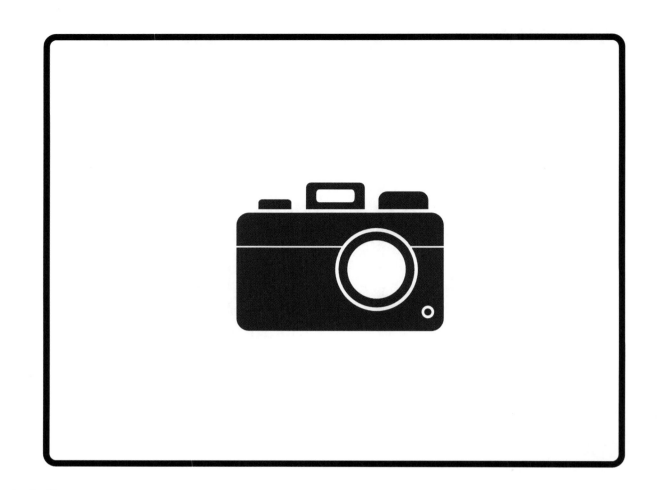

Place

Date   Title

Notes

Place

Title

Date

Notes

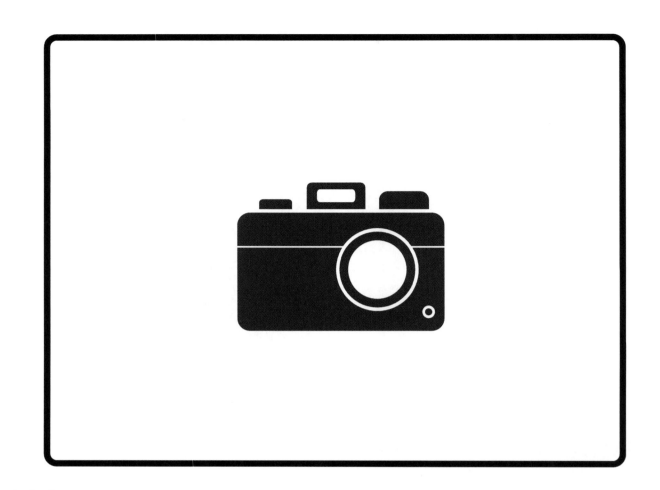

Place _____

Date _____ Title _____

Notes

Place

Title

Date

Notes

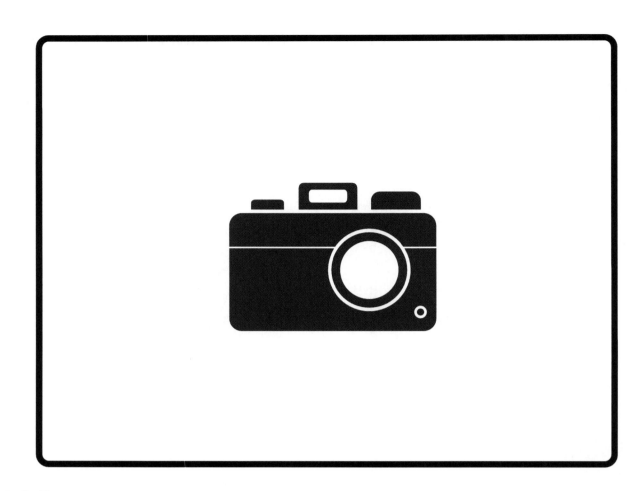

Place _____

Date _____ Title _____

Notes

_____
_____
_____
_____
_____

Place

Title

Date

Notes

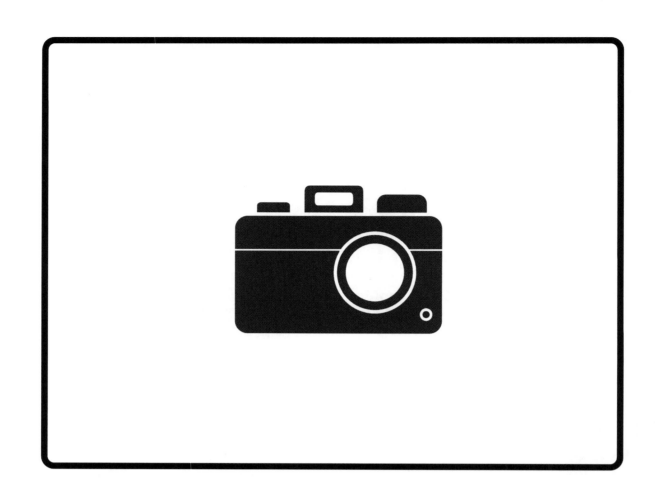

Place

Date Title

Notes

Place

Title

Date

Notes

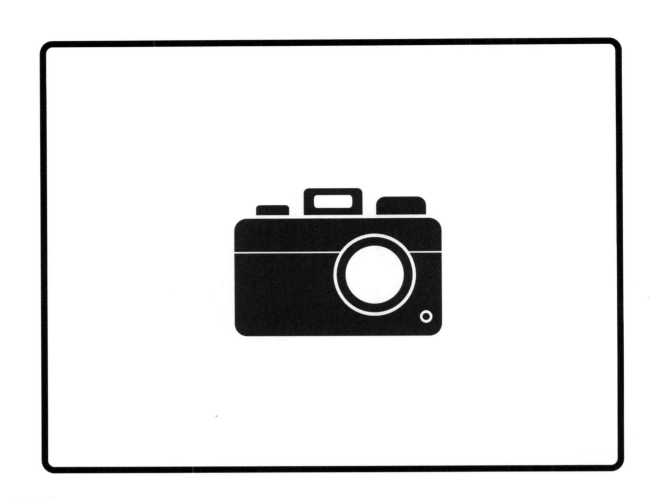

Place _____

Date _____   Title _____

Notes

_____

_____

_____

_____

_____

Place

Title

Date

Notes

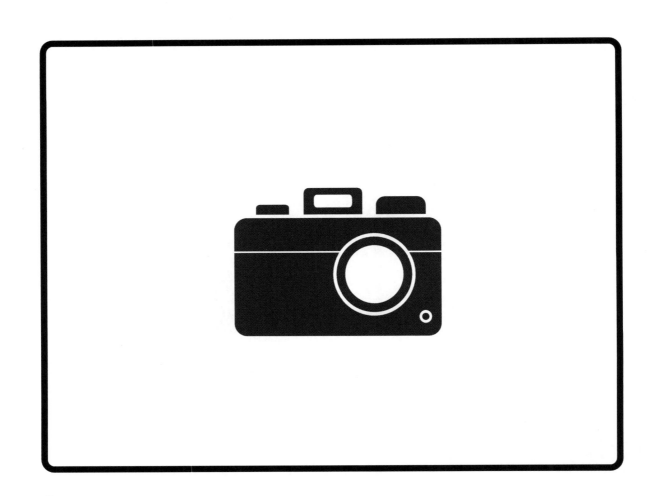

Place

Date Title

Notes

Place

Title

Date

Notes

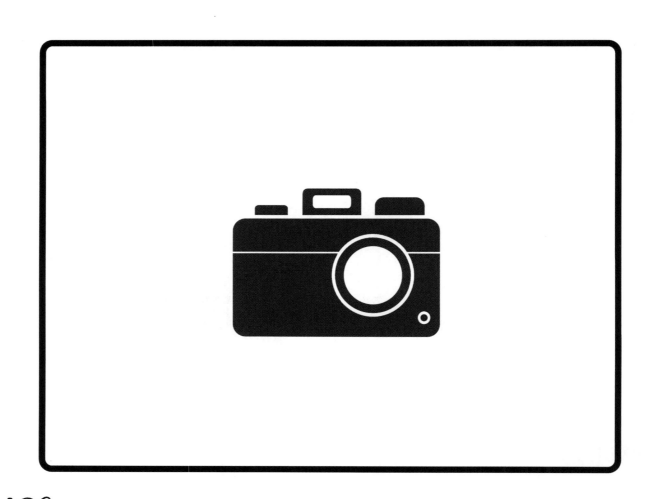

Place _____

Date _____   Title _____

Notes

_____
_____
_____
_____
_____

Place

Title

Date

Notes

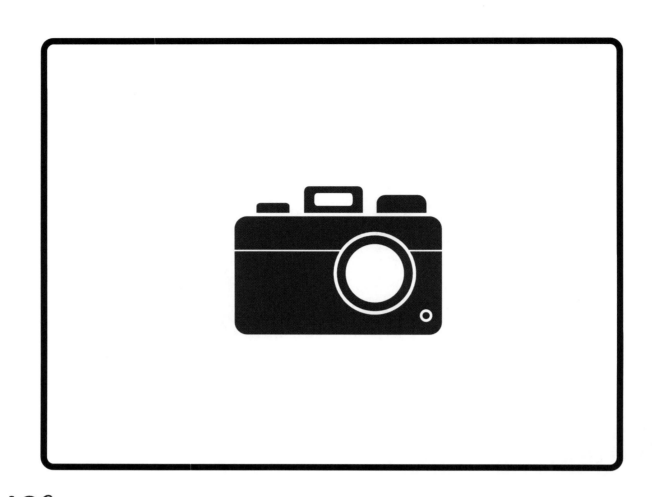

Place _____

Date _____ Title _____

Notes

_____
_____
_____
_____
_____

Place

Title

Date

Notes

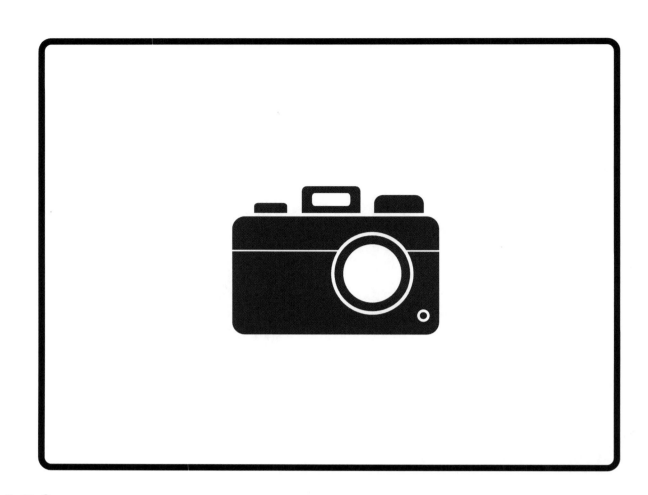

Place

Date　　　　　　　Title

Notes

Place

Title

Date

Notes

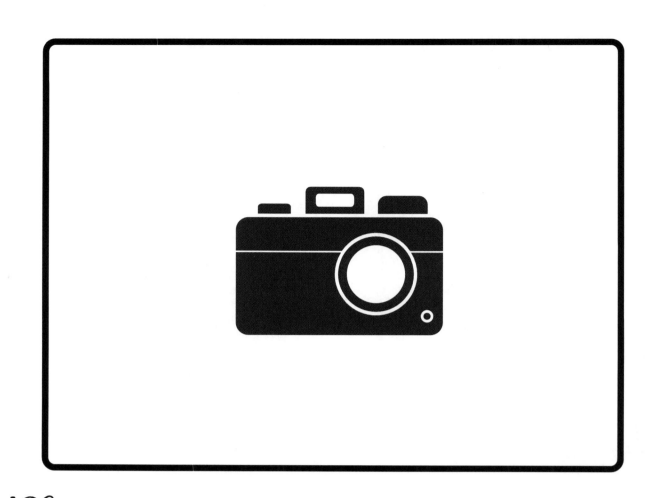

Place

Date   Title

Notes

Place

Title

Date

Notes

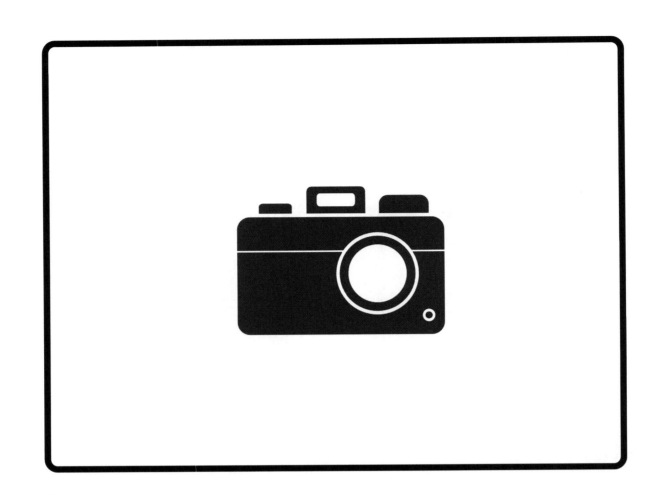

Place ___
Date ___ Title ___
Notes

Place

Title

Date

Notes

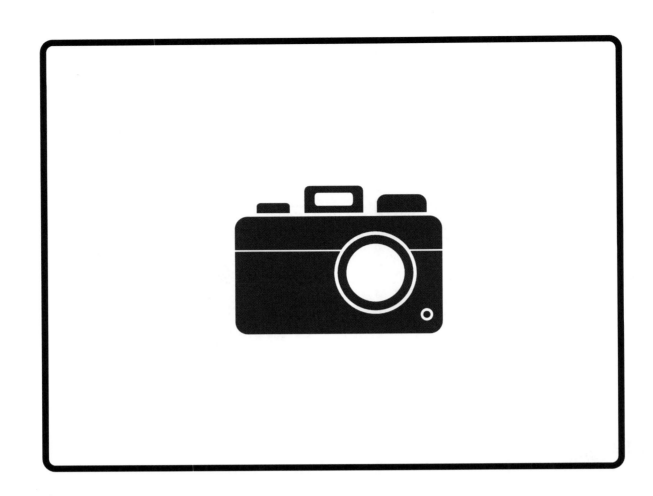

Place

Date　　　　　　　Title

Notes

Place

Title

Date

Notes

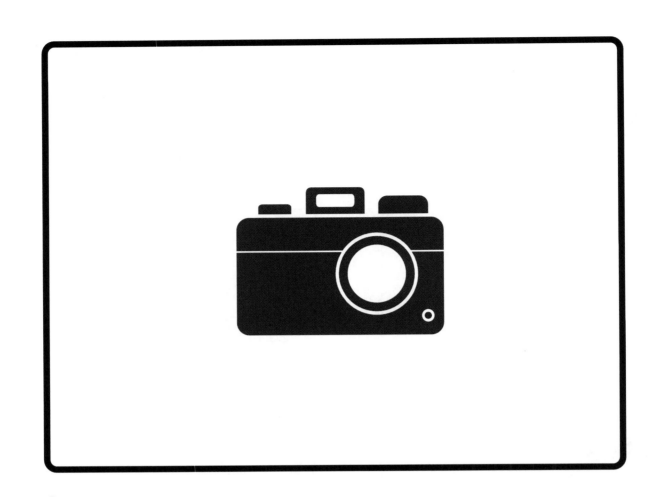

Place

Date　　　　　　　Title

Notes

Place

Title

Date

Notes

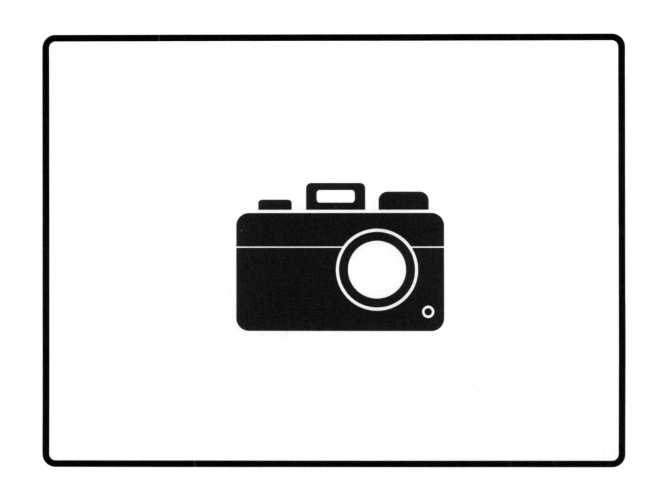

Place _____

Date _____ Title _____

Notes

_____
_____
_____
_____
_____

Place

Title

Date

Notes

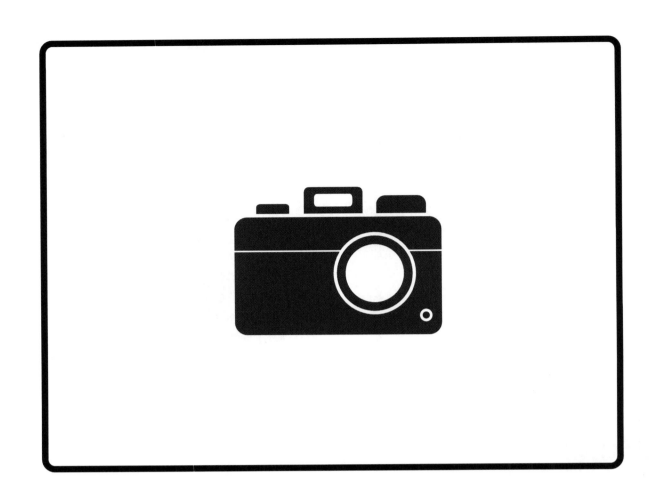

Place

Date   Title

Notes

Place

Title

Date

Notes

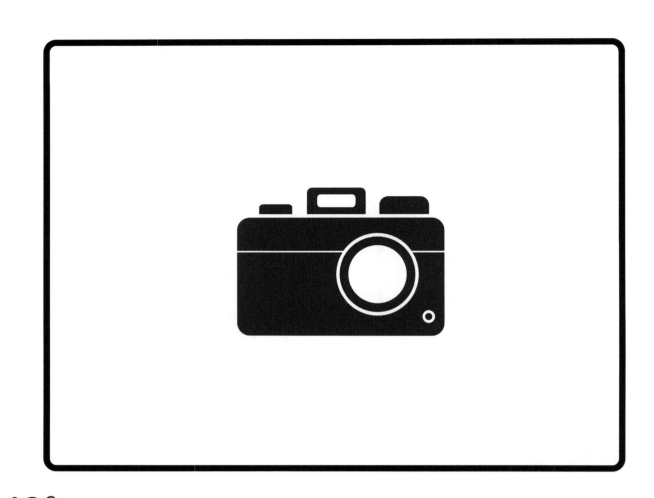

Place

Date　　　　　Title

Notes

Place

Title

Date

Notes

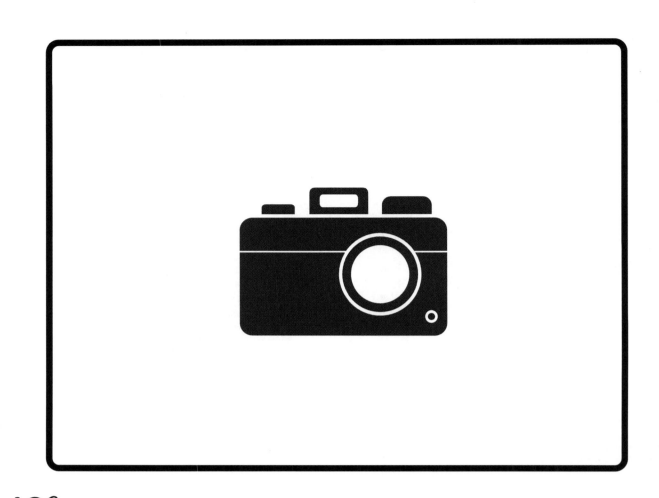

Place

Date Title

Notes

Place

Title

Date

Notes

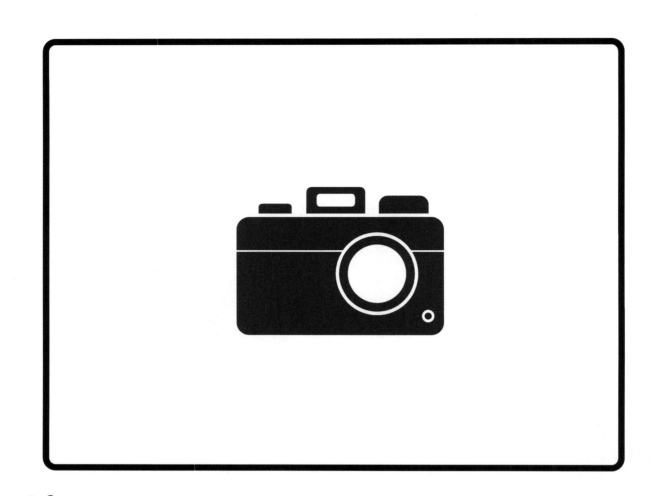

Place

Date Title

Notes

Place

Title

Date

Notes

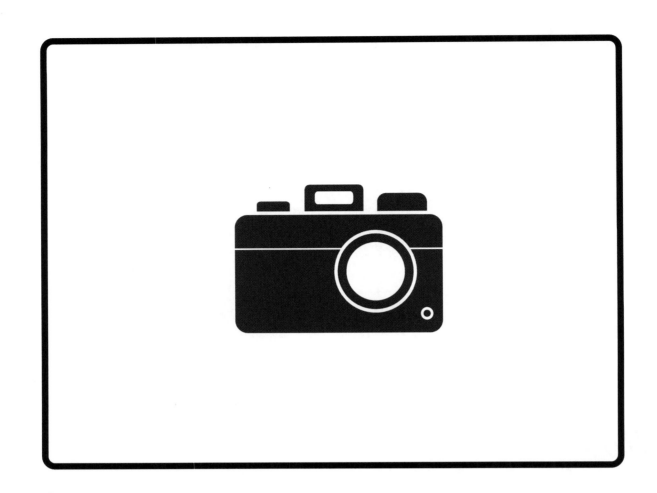

Place

Date   Title

Notes

Place

Title

Date

Notes

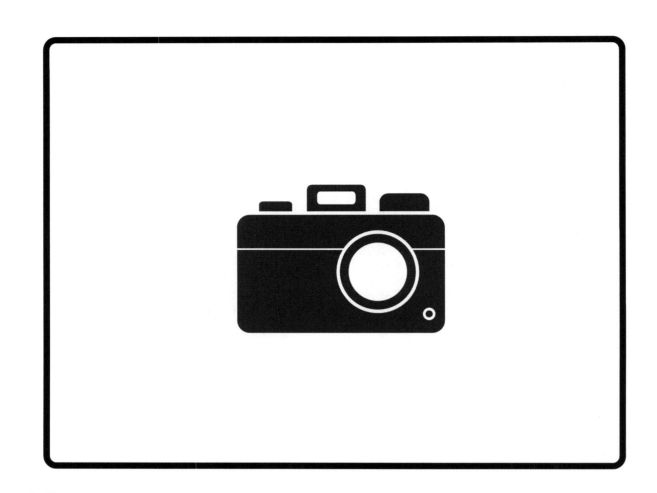

Place

Date　　　　　　　Title

Notes

Place

Title

Date

Notes

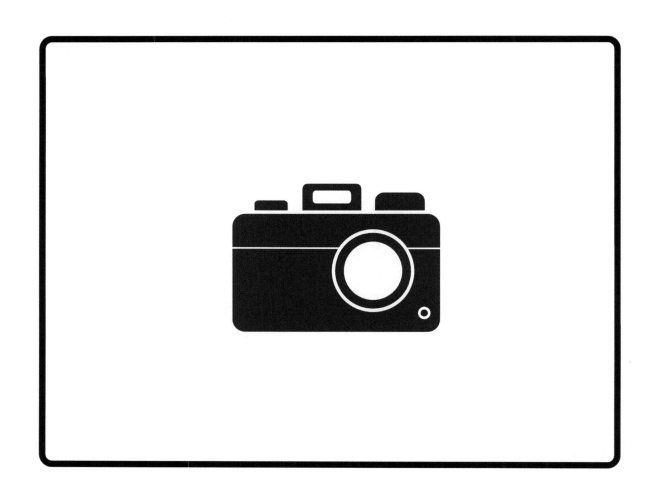

Place _____

Date _____ Title _____

Notes

_____

_____

_____

_____

_____

Printed in France by Amazon
Brétigny-sur-Orge, FR